The Statue
of Liberty

For my grandchildren—M. D. B.

To Frank and Isobel—J. G. W.

ALADDIN PAPERBACKS
An imprint of Simon & Schuster Children's Publishing Division
1230 Avenue of the Americas, New York, NY 10020
Text copyright © 2007 by Marion Dane Bauer
Illustrations copyright © 2007 by John Wallace
All rights reserved, including the right of reproduction
in whole or in part in any form.
READY-TO-READ, ALADDIN PAPERBACKS, and related logo
are registered trademarks of Simon & Schuster, Inc.
Designed by Christopher Grassi
The text of this book was set in Century Old Style.
Manufactured in the United States of America
First Aladdin Paperbacks edition September 2007
2 4 6 8 10 9 7 5 3 1
Library of Congress Cataloging-in-Publication Data
Bauer, Marion Dane.
The Statue of Liberty / by Marion Dane Bauer ;
illustrated by John Wallace.
p. cm.—(Wonders of America) (Ready-to-read)
ISBN-13: 978-1-4169-3479-0 (pbk)
ISBN-10: 1-4169-3479-0 (pbk)
ISBN-13: 978-1-4169-3480-6 (library)
ISBN-10: 1-4169-3480-4 (library)
1. Statue of Liberty (New York, N.Y.)—History—Juvenile literature.
2. New York (N.Y.)—Buildings, structures, etc.—Juvenile literature.
I. Wallace, John, 1966– ill. II. Title.
F128.64.L6B38 2007
974.7'1—dc22
2006036917

The Statue
of Liberty

By **Marion Dane Bauer**

Illustrated by **John Wallace**

Ready-to-Read
ALADDIN
New York London Toronto Sydney

A grand lady stands in
New York Harbor.
Her name is the
Statue of Liberty.

She holds a torch high
to welcome all who come
to the United States.

The Statue of Liberty
was created by a
French sculptor,
Frederic-Auguste Bartholdi.

France gave this
beautiful statue
to the United States

to honor the friendship
between the two countries.

The people of the United States
built the pedestal
to receive the statue.

American schoolchildren gave their nickels and dimes to make a place for Lady Liberty to stand.

Statue
of
Liberty

The statue is made
from sheets of copper
wrapped around a
steel structure.

She was built in France,
then taken apart and
shipped to the United States.

When she was put
together again and
set on the pedestal,
she stood 305 feet tall.

In 1886 that was taller than
any building in New York City.

When she was unveiled
thousands of people cheered.
Ships sounded their horns
and whistles.

Guns saluted.

Still today the
Statue of Liberty's
torch burns bright.

It reminds all Americans
and all who come to America
that freedom lives!

Interesting Facts about the Statue of Liberty

★ The Statue of Liberty was shipped to the United States in 350 pieces. Those pieces weighed 450,000 pounds and were packed in 214 crates.

★ The statue itself, from base to torch, is 151 feet high. The arm holding the torch is 42 feet high. Lady Liberty's index finger is 8 feet long. Her mouth is 3 feet wide.

★ It has been said that Frederic-Auguste Bartholdi modeled the statue's face after his mother's.

★ Several copies of the famous statue stand in France.

★ Bartholdi's name for his statue was *Liberty Enlightening the World*.

★ Lady Liberty has welcomed more than 12 million immigrants to the United States.

★ In 1904 a bronze tablet with a poem, "The New Colossus" by Emma Lazarus, was added to a wall of the pedestal. It includes these lines:

> *Give me your tired, your poor,*
> *Your huddled masses yearning to breathe free,*
> *The wretched refuse of your teeming shore.*
> *Send these, the homeless, tempest-tost to me,*
> *I lift my lamp beside the golden door!*